MIRACLE ON ICE

SPORTS UNITE US

Published in the United States of America by Cherry Lake Publishing
Ann Arbor, Michigan
www.cherrylakepublishing.com

Reading Adviser: Marla Conn MS, Ed., Literacy specialist, Read-Ability, Inc.

Library of Congress Cataloging-in-Publication Data has been filed and is available at catalog.loc.gov

Cherry Lake Publishing would like to acknowledge the work of The Partnership for 21st Century
Learning.
Please visit *www.p21.org* for more information.

Printed in the United States of America
Corporate Graphics

ABOUT THE AUTHOR

Heather Williams is a writer and educator with a passion for seeing readers of all ages
connect with others through stories and personal experiences. She enjoys running, reading,
and watching sports. Heather lives in Greensboro, North Carolina with her husband and
two children.

TABLE OF CONTENTS

Uneasy Times

Every four years, athletes from all over the world compete in the Winter Olympics. The Olympics are held in a different country each time. People forget about their **political** differences during the Olympics. Everyone comes together to cheer for their teams. Athletes from more than 200 countries compete for medals. There were only 16 events at the very first Winter Olympics in 1924. One of them was ice hockey. Ice hockey is a game played in three 20-minute **periods** on an ice rink. Players use curved sticks to hit a **puck** into a small goal. One of the most exciting hockey games ever played was at the 1980 Winter Olympics in Lake Placid, New York.

The threat of war with Russia created a general feeling
of gloom in America during the late 1970s.

The 1960s and 1970s were a stressful time for Americans. The
United States and Russia (then called the USSR) were not getting
along. They had been fighting about who was more powerful
since the end of World War II (1939–1945). This conflict was
called the Cold War. The Cold War was not an actual war. It
started as a disagreement over which kind of government was
better. The United States believed in **capitalism**, and Russia
preferred **communism**. The United States and Russia both
wanted to be the most powerful country in the world. The leaders
of the two countries tried to get other world leaders on their side.

The Kremlin in Moscow's Red Square has long represented Russian power and authority.

Russia threatened to use bombs and weapons to gain power. The American people were very worried about their safety. They were afraid that Russia would use **nuclear weapons** and start a war.

President Jimmy Carter was very frustrated with Russia. He decided to **boycott** the 1980 Summer Olympics in Moscow, Russia. However, Russia still went to the 1980 Winter Olympics in Lake Placid, New York. Russia saw the Olympic Games as a way to show their strength and power. The Olympics was not supposed to be political. However, both Russia and the United States could not ignore their Cold War **rivalry** during the games.

This was especially true during the Olympic ice hockey event, which Russia had dominated since 1954.

Russia saw everything, even ice hockey, as a way to promote communism. The United States viewed Russia as a "bad guy," both in politics and in sports. So the people of both countries had good reasons for watching the game between the two teams on February 22, 1980.

Capitalism and Communism

Communism is a type of government. A communist government controls the country's **resources**. *The government is supposed to provide enough money, food, and clothing for everyone. Capitalism is also a type of government. Capitalism involves a free market and less government control. That means citizens in a capitalist country earn and spend their own money. They buy the things they need, such as food and clothes.*

Gods on Ice

Russia won its first Olympic medal for ice hockey in 1956. After the 1956 Winter Olympics, Russia was the best Olympic ice hockey team for 30 years. They only lost the gold medal twice during that time. Both times, they lost to the United States.

The Russian ice hockey team was chosen and trained by the government. They trained for many hours a day. They were coached by the best ice hockey coaches and players in Russia. The Olympics did not allow **professional** athletes to compete. Russia gave its ice hockey players job titles or **military** assignments. But they did not really do those jobs. Instead, they practiced ice hockey all day. They practiced as much as professional ice hockey players in the United States and Canada. They were pushed to

The USSR won the World Ice Hockey Championships for the fifth-straight year in 1967.

become the best players in the world. Even though they were considered **amateurs**, they played like pros. Russia's ice hockey team was nicknamed "The Red Machine."

Russia developed its own style of playing ice hockey. It was very different from the way ice hockey was played in Canada and the United States. The team was also in really good shape. Other teams could not keep up with Russia's speed, stamina, and long passes across the ice. In February 1979, the Russian ice hockey team played a **tournament** against the National Hockey League (NHL) **All-Star** team. It was called the Challenge Cup. The NHL

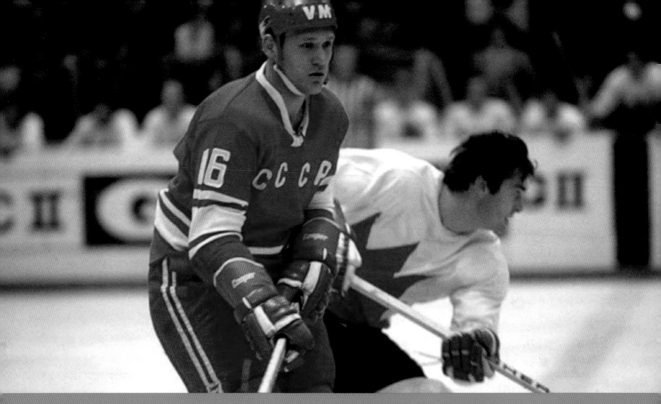

The Russian ice hockey team's size and experience earned
them the nickname "The Red Machine."

All-Star team was made up of the best professional hockey players
from Canada and the United States. Russia lost the first game
4–2, but dominated the other two games and won the
tournament.

The U.S. played Russia a few weeks before the 1980 Olympics
in an exhibition, or practice game. More than 11,000 people
showed up to see the match. The U.S. team was in awe of the
larger and more experienced Russian players. They remembered
how Russia had beaten a group of professional hockey players in

the Challenge Cup. The American team seemed to be watching the Russians instead of playing against them. During the third period, Russia scored three goals in three minutes. Russia's coach claimed that his team did not even play their best. Russia beat the U.S. team 10–3. The two teams would have to meet again just a few weeks later. After the exhibition game, no one expected the U.S. team to win a gold medal at the Olympics. Everyone expected Russia to dominate the event, just as they had for nearly 30 years.

Bandy

Before Russia discovered ice hockey, Russians played a game called bandy. It shares some similarities with ice hockey. It is played on an ice rink, and players use curved sticks. It also shares many similarities with soccer. Instead of a puck, players try to hit a ball into the goal. The **goalkeeper** does not use a stick. Instead, the goalkeeper can pick up the ball with his or her hands.

Unlikely Heroes

In the summer of 1979, Coach Herb Brooks tried out 68 of some of America's best young ice hockey players. Brooks put the players through long, difficult drills. He made them take a 300-question psychological test. Brooks was not just looking for good ice hockey players. He wanted players who were flexible and willing to learn new ways to play ice hockey. Brooks also wanted players who could handle his high demands. He chose 20 players for the Olympic team.

The athletes Coach Brooks chose were mostly young college players. The average age of the U.S. ice hockey team was 21. It was the youngest Olympic hockey team in the history of the Olympics. Many of them were from rival college teams. They

Coach Herb Brooks motivated his players with fear and a demand for perfection.

held **grudges** and fought with each other at first. Coach Brooks decided to be so hard on them that they would come together in their dislike for him. He told them he was not there to be their friend. They soon began to unite and play together as a team.

Coach Brooks taught the team a new style of playing that was similar to how the Russian team played. He made them skate sprints on the ice until they couldn't stand up. The players called these sprints "Herbies," after the coach. Every time they lost or tied a game, Coach Brooks made them skate Herbies. They

Goalkeeper Jim Craig celebrates the U.S. victory on the ice at the Olympic field house in Lake Placid, New York.

became better, stronger ice hockey players. More importantly, they became a family.

Nicknamed "Rizzo," Mike Eruzione was the captain of the 1980 U.S. Olympic team. He played ice hockey at Boston University. Eruzione scored the winning goal in the Olympic game against Russia. After the Olympics, he retired from ice hockey. Eruzione later became a **motivational speaker**.

Jim Craig's performance as goalkeeper in the game against Russia is legendary. He stopped 36 out of 39 of Russia's shots.

Craig played ice hockey at Boston University. He said he decided to play goalie because he didn't know the rules for the other positions. Craig played in the NHL for a few years before retiring from ice hockey.

All-Time Olympic Hockey Medal Count

	Russia (including USSR)		United States of America
🥇	7	Gold	2
🥈	2	Silver	8
🥉	2	Bronze	1

Buzz Schneider was the only member of the U.S. team who had played on the 1976 Olympic team. At 25, he was the oldest member of the 1980 team. Schneider played left wing, a position responsible for scoring. He scored the first goal in the game against Russia. After the Olympics, Schneider played in the NHL until 1982.

Total Hockey

Coach Herb Brooks taught his team a whole new way to play hockey. He borrowed a method made famous by Dutch professional soccer teams. It was known as total football. The style of play forced players to learn more than one position. They were used to staying in one position and waiting for the puck to come to them. Russia was famous for using a total hockey style of play. Brooks taught his team to use Russia's own method to defeat them.

The Right Man for the Job

Coach Herb Brooks played hockey at the University of Minnesota. He was cut from the U.S. ice hockey team a few days before the 1960 Olympics. Another player's face was pasted over his in the team photo. That team went on to defeat Russia and win a gold medal. Brooks watched the game on television. Later, he became the coach of the U.S. ice hockey team. Brooks had always regretted not playing on the 1960 gold-medal team. He had a very personal reason for wanting the U.S. team to beat Russia in 1980. Brooks was very demanding and often harsh. He pushed his players to their limits. Brooks hardly ever gave his players compliments. Inside, he was very proud of them. Brooks was very emotional after the win against Russia. While everyone else was celebrating, he went to the locker room and cried.

Do You Believe in Miracles?

The Olympic field house was overflowing on the evening of February 22, 1980. For the American people, the game was about more than ice hockey. The game was a **symbol** of everything happening in the world. Americans needed to feel excited and happy about something. Even people who didn't know anything about ice hockey were watching the U.S. team play Russia. Families were gathered around their televisions. People were listening on their car radios. The U.S. team was just a bunch of kids. The Russian players were bigger, faster, and more experienced. But America was hoping for a miracle.

The Russians took the lead early, but the United States tied the score with a goal from Buzz Schneider. Close to the end of the first period, the Russian team led 2–1. With one second left in the

Lake Placid's Olympic field house, the site of the famous "Miracle on Ice," was renamed Herb Brooks Arena in 2005 after the U.S. Men's coach.

period, Mark Johnson scored. The game was tied again. The Russian coach was so angry that he took his star goalkeeper out of the game. During the second period, the Russians only scored once. The United States remained behind Russia with a score of 3–2. The entire country was glued to the game as the third period started.

The U.S. team tied the score 3–3 eight minutes into the third period with another goal by Mark Johnson. Everyone in the Olympic field house was on their feet. Fans at the game and people watching on television were chanting "U-S-A! U-S-A!" With 10 minutes left in the game, captain Mike Eruzione scored, and the United States took the lead. During the final 10 minutes of the game, the Russian team went on the attack. But the United States did not back down, and Russia began to make mistakes. Russia did not manage to score again. As the final seconds of the game ticked away, announcer Al Michaels counted down and spoke his now famous words, "Do you believe in miracles?" When the buzzer sounded, the field house went wild.

Going for Gold

The United States win against Russia was special for America. But the U.S. team still had another game to play. While the rest of the country celebrated Russia's defeat, the team was preparing to play Finland. If the U.S. team lost to Finland, there was a chance they would not win a medal at all. Beating Finland guaranteed the United States the gold. The United States ended up winning the gold medal game 4–2. They were truly the "greatest team in the world."

In the final moments of the game, the United States did
not back down and Russia could not recover.

Team USA shakes hands with a stunned Russian team after the semifinal game.

At first, the U.S. ice hockey team did not understand the significance of their win. For them, it was just about beating a legendary team. But they became symbols of hope for the American people. They are still known today for the miracle they pulled off in 1980.

[21ST CENTURY SKILLS LIBRARY]

A Call for the Ages

Al Michaels is known for his famous countdown call at the end of the United States vs. Russia ice hockey game where he said, "Do you believe in miracles?" Michaels was chosen to call the game because he was the only ABC announcer who had ever called an ice hockey game. He had called only one ice hockey game in the past, in the 1972 Winter Olympics. He had no experience playing ice hockey, but he got the job because he had been an ice hockey fan as a child. Michaels says his emotional call was completely **spontaneous**. If he had thought about it, he says he might not have said it at all. He was afraid it sounded too corny. Instead, he got caught up in the excitement and emotion of the game. The call is now one of the most famous sports moments of all time.

CHAPTER 5

Out of Many, One

America celebrated their ice hockey team's win over Russia. Across the country, people rushed into the streets. Drivers listening in their cars pulled over and danced around with total strangers. People hugged each other and cried tears of happiness. The national anthem was sung in stores, on streets, and in living rooms. A ship called the USS Nimitz flashed the score of the game to a nearby Russian ship. The defeat of the Red Machine meant a great deal to America. The win was a symbol of what could be. The Russian team stood for the powerful giant Americans feared. And the U.S. team stood for everything that was good about America. They were clean-cut boys from good families. They believed in hard work and loved their country.

More than 8,000 people squeezed into the Olympic field house to watch Team USA defeat Russia.

The game was the miracle the United States needed. It gave the American people hope.

After the game, the Russian players watched the U.S. team celebrate. Some of them were even smiling. One of the players said he was happy for the Americans. In the locker room, the U.S. team sang "God Bless America" together. The wall outside the U.S. locker room was covered with telegrams from people congratulating the team.

Captain Mike Eruzione invited the entire team to join him on the winner's podium at the gold medal ceremony.

At the medal ceremony, only captain Mike Eruzione stood on the podium. But when he received his medal, he called his team over. Twenty hockey players tried to stand together on a podium meant for one person. The team had become what Coach Brooks meant for them to be: a family. By bringing them together, he managed to unite an entire country. They were invited to the White House so President Carter could congratulate them in person. The entire team was named Sports Illustrated Sportsmen of the Year for 1980. They had done something no one in America thought possible at the time. They had defeated Russia.

The Cold War officially ended in 1991. After the Cold War, many Russian ice hockey players came to America to play in the NHL. Many of the 1980 Olympic rivals became teammates. In 2002, 22 years later, the 1980 men's hockey team lit the Olympic torch at the Winter Olympics in Salt Lake City, Utah. It was the first time an entire team lit the torch. They were still a family, and they were still a symbol of what America could be.

The End of the Cold War

The USSR was a large communist country. It was made up of 15 smaller countries. In the late 1980s, the people of the USSR decided they were tired of living under communism. They fought to win back their individual countries. In 1991, the USSR broke apart. There were 15 individual, independent countries again. With the end of the USSR came the end of the Cold War.

TIMELINE

FEBRUARY 9

The United States completes pre-Olympic play with a 10–3 loss to the Russian team.

SEPTEMBER 3

The U.S. team begins its pre-Olympics tour in Europe with a game against the Netherlands.

SEPTEMBER 30

The team loses the first of three games against NHL teams.

1980

1979

AUGUST

Coach Brooks holds tryouts in Colorado Springs, Colorado, at the National Sports Festival.

FEBRUARY 12

The United States ties Sweden on the opening day of the 1980 Winter Olympics in Lake Placid, New York.

FEBRUARY 20

The United States defeats West Germany 4–2.

FEBRUARY 16

The United States defeats Norway 5–1.

FEBRUARY 24

The United States wins the gold medal after defeating Finland 4–2.

FEBRUARY 14

The United States defeats Czechoslovakia 7–3.

FEBRUARY 22

In the game now known as "The Miracle on Ice," the United States defeats Russia 4–3.

FEBRUARY 18

The United States defeats Romania 7–2.

Think About It

What is happening in this photo? Why is it important to the team? To Coach Herb Brooks? To America?

What can you learn about the U.S. men's ice hockey team from this picture?

At tryouts the year before the Olympics, many of the players were from rival college teams and did not get along. Why was it important for them to forget about their differences and become like a family? What specific events and experiences brought them to this moment?

[21ST CENTURY SKILLS LIBRARY]

Learn More

BOOKS

Labrecque, Ellen. *Ice Hockey*. Ann Arbor, MI: Cherry Lake Publishing, 2018.

Taylor, David. *The Cold War*. Chicago: Heinemann Library, 2001.

Trusdell, Brian. *The Miracle on Ice*. Minneapolis: Sportszone, 2015.

ON THE WEB

The Cold War for Kids
www.ducksters.com/history/cold_war/summary.php

The Official Home Page of the Olympic Games
www.olympic.org/lake-placid-1980

The U.S. Hockey Hall of Fame: The 1980 U.S. Olympic Team
www.ushockeyhalloffame.com/page/show/831562-the-1980-u-s-Olympic-team

GLOSSARY

All-Star (AHL-stahr) an outstanding performer or athlete

amateurs (A-muh-churz) people who are not paid for a job or activity (athletes who play a sport for fun)

boycott (BOI-kaht) to refuse to do business with a person, business, or country in order to show disapproval

capitalism (KAP-ih-tuh-lih-zum) an economic system that allows people and companies to make decisions about money and own property

communism (KAH-myoo-nih-zum) an economic system in which the government owns all companies and property and makes all decisions about money

goalkeeper (GOHL-kee-pur) the player on a hockey team who stands in front of the goal and tries to keep the other team from scoring

grudges (GRUH-jihz) anger or dislike between two people that lasts a very long time

military (MIH-lih-tehr-ee) anything related to soldiers, weapons, or war

motivational speaker (moh-tih-VAY-shuh-nul SPEE-ker) someone who makes speeches to inspire a group of people

nuclear weapons (NOO-clee-ur WEH-punz) weapons of mass destruction that are powered by a sudden release of atomic energy

periods (PEE-ree-uhdz) the three 20-minute segments of a hockey game

political (puh-LIH-tih-kul) relating to the actions of government

professional (pruh-FEH-shuh-nul) someone who is paid for a job or activity (an athlete who is paid to play a sport)

puck (PUK) a black rubber disk that hockey players try to hit into a goal

resources (REE-sor-sez) things like land, money, and food that people need to live

rivalry (RAI-vul-ree) intense competition between two people or teams

spontaneous (spahn-TAY-nee-us) happening suddenly

symbol (SIM-bul) an object, person, or group that stands for an idea

tournament (TUR-nuh-mehnt) a series of games where one person or team advances to a final and wins a trophy or title

INDEX